Roger Federer Retires: His biography, records and why he retired

Eddie Brock

Table of Contents

- Chapter 1

- Chapter 2

Chapter 1

Life of Roger Federer and his records

Roger Federer, (conceived on August 8, 1981, in Basel, Switzerland) was a Swiss tennis player who overwhelmed the game in the mid 21st 100 years with his outstanding overall game. He likewise has a blended legacy (and double citizenship) - his dad is Swiss and his mother is South African. He grew up playing different games notwithstanding tennis, like football, badminton, and b-ball. Federer used to be a firebrand in his initial years, however as his profession advanced he procured the standing of being ice-cool on the court. Many credits change to the demise of Federer's long-lasting mentor Peter Carter (in 2002, to a fender bender). The misfortune influenced Federer in an extraordinary arrangement, and his disposition turned out to be recognizably more settled afterward.

Federer has one kin, his more established sister Diana, who is the mother of a bunch of twins. He experienced childhood in neighboring Birsfelden, Riehen, and afterward Münchenstein, near the French and German boundaries, and speaks Swiss German, Standard German, English, and French easily, Swiss German being his local language.

Brought up as a Roman Catholic, he started playing tennis and soccer at an early age. However everybody in his family partook in the game, it was youthful Federer who showed the commitment to becoming wildly successful. When he turned 11, he became one of the Main 3 Junior Tennis Players in Switzerland.

He focused his energies on tennis alone, abandoning any remaining games. He began playing competitions, rehearsing and molding himself to turn into a pro at just the age of 14. From that point, he secured the Public Junior Title in Switzerland. His huge ability and playing abilities procured him a sponsorship at the Swiss Public Tennis Community in Ecublens. No sooner than 1996, he was a member of the Worldwide Tennis Organization junior tennis circuit.

Turning proficient, his most memorable match was against Lucas Arnold Ker in Gstaad, Switzerland which he lost. However, he had previously secured himself in beginner tennis, duplicating the achievement expertly demanded investment and experience. Federer won the Wimbledon young men's singles and doubles titles in 1998 and turned professional soon thereafter. Likewise in 1998, preceding sending off himself expertly, he made some meaningful difference as a beginner by coming out on top for the lesser Wimbledon championship and the Orange Bowl, accordingly becoming perceived as the ITF World Junior Tennis Boss of the Year.

At Wimbledon in 2001, he created an uproar by taking out reigning singles champion Pete Sampras in the fourth round. In 2003, following an effective season on grass, Federer turned into the primary Swiss man to come out on top for a Huge home run championship when he rose successfully at Wimbledon.

In 2003, Federer laid out the Roger Federer Establishment, which gives awards to unfortunate nations that have kid death paces of more than 15%, for schooling and sports-related projects, among others.

Toward the start of 2004, he won the Australian Open, the U.S. Open, the ATP Bosses, held the Wimbledon singles title, and had a world positioning of No. 2. That very year, he was positioned No. 1 toward the beginning of 2005 and his victories that year incorporated the Wimbledon singles title (for a third progressive year) and the U.S. Open.

The year 2005 got off to a horrendous start as he lost two Huge home run titles. Notwithstanding, he before long recovered, winning the Wimbledon and the US Open. Besides, his series of wins at the four ATP Experts Series 1000 and two ATP 500 series proceeded, which assisted him in withholding his no.1 position. In 2006, his capability at the game transcended the aptitude of his rivals, as he went on to come out on top for three Huge homerun singles championships. Furthermore, he won four of the ATP Bosses Series 1000 finals and one out of the two ATP 500 series. He made a full go-around by coming to the World no. 1 situation for a third time frame in succession.

2007 was an imitation of 2006, all things considered, as he once more came to the finals of each of the four, winning three toward the end. All things considered, he won five while in the ATP 500 series he won one. He got the no. 1 status for a fourth time frame, in this manner essentially ruling the game. In 2008, Federer beat Scottish player Andy Murray in the U.S. Open — his fifth U.S. Open win. In any case, that year ended up being a troublesome time in Federer's vocation: He lost to equal Rafael Nadal at both the French Open and Wimbledon, and lost to one more youthful star, Novak Djokovic, at the 2008 Australian Open. His positioning additionally slid to No. 2 without precedent for four years.

In June 2009 Federer won his most memorable French Open, giving him a title in every one of the four Huge home run competitions throughout his vocation. Also, the success was his fourteenth Huge home run title, which tied Federer with Sampras for the most in all time. The next month at Wimbledon, Federer crushed American Andy Roddick in an exhilarating long-distance race five-set match (5-7, 7-6, 7-6, 3-6, 16-14) to come out on top for his 6th Wimbledon title and his record fifteenth vocation Huge home run title; he in this manner recovered the world number one positioning. In January 2010 he won the Australian Open, overcoming Andy Murray of Extraordinary England. Federer again crushed Murray in 2012 to win his record-tying seventh vocation Wimbledon title. After a month the two men went head to head in the gold decoration match at the London Olympics. This time, nonetheless, Federer lost to Murray and needed to make do with silver decoration.

The destruction in his profession diagram went on as he neglected to pack a solitary title at the four Huge home runs for the year 2011, his most memorable time beginning around 2002. His reality positioning gradually plated further as he exited the best 3. What appeared to be a title-less year finished on a high note as he killed the dry season brought about by winning the Swiss Inside his fifth time and his presentation Paris Experts title.

During the 2011 ATP visit, he restored his sinking vocation by overcoming David Ferrer to arrive at the last at the year-end titles for the seventh time, which was his 100th last. It was his exhibition at the ATP Visit that assisted him with recovering the no.3 positioning.

Yet again Federer's vocation was raised in 2012 when he crushed Andy Murray for a record-tying seventh Wimbledon singles title. The triumph assisted the 30-year-old tennis player's return to the No. 1 spot, and before the year's over he had laid out a record with a sum of 302 weeks on the world rankings.

In 2013, Federer made an unexpected takeoff from Wimbledon. He was taken out of the singles rivalry in the second round by Sergiy Stakhovsky, who was positioned 116th at that point. At the U.S. Open, Federer again battled on the court. He was knocked out by Spain's Tommy Robredo losing in three straight sets in the 4th round.

Federer struggled against Djokovic in the 2014 men's singles last at Wimbledon, however, was denied a record eighth title on the popular grass courts in a five-set misfortune. He then, at that point, lost in the elimination rounds of the U.S. Open to hard-hitting Croatian Marin Cilic, who proceeded to win the competition.

Federer's 2015 season started on a disheartening note with a misfortune to Italy's Andreas Seppi in the third round of the Australian Open. He demonstrated he may as yet rival the game's top players by overcoming Djokovic to come out on top for the Dubai Titles in February, yet his brief French Open crown was defeated with a quarterfinal misfortune to kinsman Stan Wawrinka.

Federer charged through the draw at Wimbledon a month after the fact, however, he was crushed in the last by Djokovic, postponing his journey for a record eighth title for essentially one more year. His destiny was something similar at the U.S. Open: Regardless of an amazing appearance that recommended professional Huge Grand slam title No. 18 was coming, Federer essentially couldn't move beyond the highest level Djokovic in a hard-battled last.

Before the 2016 Australian Open, he played in a record 65th back-to-back Huge Grand Slam competition. At the 2015 US Open, he achieved a record 27th Huge Grand slam last. Before the 2013 French Open, Federer arrived at a record 36th continuous Huge Grand slam quarterfinal. Federer has won the most matches on Huge Grand slam occasions (312) and is quick to record 65+ successes at every Huge Grand slam competition. This expert tennis player is prominently alluded to as Taken care of Express or FedEx. Individuals even call him Swiss Maestro or Maestro for his remarkable abilities at the game.

In July 2016, Federer didn't come to the Wimbledon finals by the same token. He was crushed in five sets by Milos Raonic in a memorable triumph for Raonic, who turned into the primary Canadian man to arrive at a huge Grand slam last. Prior that year Federer lost the Australian Open to Novak Djokovic, and after their co-ordination, Federer was sidelined with a knee injury. Later in the season, Federer experienced back issues, and he had to pull out from the French Open to stay away from additional injury.

Federer additionally played in the Hopman Cup and Australian Open in January 2017. At the Australian Open, he beat top-10 players Tomáš Berdych and Kei Nishikori to arrive at the quarterfinals, where he beat Mischa Zverev, making Federer the most established man to contend in a huge homerun semi-last since Jimmy Connors in 1991.

A top competitor, Federer is an all-court, all-over player known for his speed, liquid style of play, and excellent shot-making. Federer fundamentally plays from the gauge but at the same time is agreeable at the net, being one of the most mind-blowing volleyers in the game today. He has a strong, exact crush and successfully performs uncommon components in the present tennis, for example, strike crush and skyhook, half-volley, and bounce crush (sure thing). David Cultivate Wallace looked at the savage power of Federer's forehand movement with that of "an extraordinary fluid whip", while John McEnroe alluded to Federer's forehand as "the best shot in our game." Federer is likewise known for his proficient development around the court and great footwork, which empowers him to go around shots coordinated to his strike and on second thought hit a strong back to front or inside-in forehand, quite possibly of his absolute best.

His most memorable serve is regularly around 200 km/h (125 mph); in any case, he is equipped for serving at 220 km/h (137 mph). Federer is likewise achieved at serve and volleying and utilized this strategy habitually in his initial profession.

Federer attached the matrimonial bunch with tennis player Mirka Vavrinec, a previous individual from the Ladies' Tennis Relationship on April 11, 2009, whom he met during the 2000 Olympics in Sydney. Vavrinec resigned from the visit in 2002 because of a foot injury. The couple has two arrangements of indistinguishable twins - twin young ladies brought into the world in 2009, and twin young men brought into the world in 2014. The whole Federer family - his folks Robert and Lynette, spouse Mirka and the Federer kids Myla Rose, Charlene Riva, Lenny, and Leo - are in many cases found in the stands during his matches, applauding him.

Roger Federer has, for the last 10 years and a half, been a close ideal envoy of tennis. Victor of a record 20 Huge home runs and holder of different records, the Swiss maestro has transformed a whole age into lovers and carried even relaxed watchers into the overlap of tennis being a fan. Federer's slick play and noble way of behaving have upgraded his standing considerably further, to the point that he was once cast a ballot as the second generally regarded person on the planet (after Nelson Mandela).

Federer is a forceful player who likes to take the ball on the ascent and finish early. Even though he began as an all-courter, bringing home his most memorable Wimbledon championship generally from the forecourt, he withdrew to the standard as the game bit by bit turned out to be less helpful for hard and fast assault. Federer's forehand is his prevailing wing, and he grants a colossal measure of topspin to it with a flighty hold. It is viewed as perhaps of the best forehand throughout the entire existence of tennis, and quite possibly of the most horrendous weapon at any point seen on the court. Federer's strike, a one-hander, is notable for its tastefulness and excellence yet has been uncovered as a responsibility by players who assault it with a lot of twists and bob - most strikingly Rafael Nadal. He has further developed it throughout the long term, significantly releasing a large number of strike victors to win the 2017 Australian Open, however it stays the most vulnerable piece of his game.

The service is a significant weapon in Federer's arms stockpile. Even though he can't match the speed that the goliaths of the game like John Isner and Ivo Karlovic can produce, Federer's mask, precision, and variety assist him with winning a lot of free places in pretty much every match. Federer's protective capacities have declined throughout the long term. While he used to be exceptionally speedy around the court during his heyday, as of late he has depended more on reflexes and expectation while attempting to fight off more grounded adversaries.

The Federer versus Nadal contention is perhaps the most discussed story throughout the entire existence of tennis. Nadal was the main player to mount a serious test to Federer's mastery, and to this date has a high ground in the no holds barred count. The two have shared numerous amazing fights throughout their professions. The Federer-Nadal last at Wimbledon 2008 is generally viewed as the best match ever, and there has even been a narrative named 'Brilliant ideas' made on it. Federer's inheritance, be that as it may, is generally free of his match-ups and battles against individual greats Nadal and Djokovic. During Federer's top, from 2004 to 2007, his matchless quality was almost outright; he was positioned No. 1 in every one of those years and won 11 out of a potential 16 Rams during the stunning run. That makes him potentially the most remarkable boss throughout the entire existence of men's tennis; no other player has at any point had such a supported run of strength in the game.

What's more, Federer's imaginative style of play has earned him acclamations from the two specialists and fans. He is a very rare example of competitors to have joined easy elegance with especially steady outcomes. What's more, the way that he has done such while soothing himself with poise both on and off the court has charmed him to the world at large; he is the group most loved any place he goes. Federer is likewise very popular among his friends, having won the Stefan Edberg Sportsmanship grant (which is decided in favor of by all the ATP players) a record multiple times. His completion of 17 professional men's singles Huge Grand Slam titles is the most in tennis history.

Seen by tennis intellectuals as the best player ever, Federer is known for his brief speed, liquid play, and outstanding shot-making. His power-stuffed crushes, brilliant footwork, and productive methods made him win matches as well as make history. He holds a record of being the main player to hold the no. 1 situation for a considerable length of time in general, out of which 237 weeks were for a stretch from 2004 until 2008. He stayed in the Main 2 for a considerable length of time on the run, from 2003 to 2010, and in the Top 3 from 2003 until 2012.

He has the differentiation of being one among the seven tennis players on the planet to have a lifelong Huge Grandslam. From 2003 until 2012, he was congratulated by the Fans' Number one Honor from the ATPWorldTour.com. His partners, opponents, and contenders have cast a ballot for him for the Stefan Edberg Sportsmanship Grant for a record multiple times, from 2004 until 2009, in 2011, and 2012. He is likewise the pleased beneficiary of the Laureus World Athlete of the Year grant for a record multiple times, from 2005 to 2008. In 2006, he was likewise met with the Arthur Ashe Philanthropic of the Year Grant.

Moreover, he has accumulated a sum of 17 Huge Grand slam titles to date. This separated, he is the pleased beneficiary of an

Olympic gold award and silver decoration for duplicates and singles individually.

Chapter 2

Reasons why Roger Federer retired

Only a short time after Serena Williams played her last match at the US Open, another tennis symbol is calling it a profession: Roger Federer as of late took to his Instagram to report that the impending Laver Cup would be his last event. Yet another tennis legend is calling it a vocation. He arrived at his choice at 41 by accomplishing something intriguing for him: surrendering — to an extended time of calm stressing to recapture first-class structure after a fourth knee medical procedure beginning around 2016 arrived behind schedule the previous summer. The tennis legend is one of the most achieved tennis players of his age, yet throughout the entire existence of the game when comes to Swiss tennis players. He came out on top for

20 Huge homerun singles championships, third to Rafael Nadal (22) and Novak Djokovic (21) - - both of whom are as yet dynamic.

In a proclamation on his Twitter account, Federer tweeted that this year's Laver Cup in London, which will be held from September 23rd to 25th will be his last proficient competition. The 41-year-old tennis legend referred to injury issues as one of the principal reasons he will quit playing.

As a lot of you know, the past three years have been tough on me with issues such as wounds and medical procedures, he tweeted. As the strong person I've always been, I've done all I can to get back on my feet and full body capacity with all seriousness. Be that as it may, I likewise know my body's abilities and cutoff points, and its message to me recently has been clear. Tennis has treated me more liberally than I at any point would have envisioned, and presently I should perceive when the time has come to end my cutthroat vocation."

Federer added that while the Laver Cup will be his last occasion on the ATP visit, he "will play more tennis later on," however not "in Huge home runs or on the visit." Federer was positioned as world No. 1 for a long time in his vocation, and that incorporates at one point for a record 237 successive weeks. He was just 21 when he won his most memorable significant singles Huge home run at Wimbledon in 2003. He went on to win that tournament several times, including catching it multiple times in succession from the year 2003-2007.

Addressing a message to "the fans who give the game its life," Federer said, "I've endeavored to get back to full serious structure, however, I likewise know my body's abilities as at the age of 41. Tennis has always been a source of hope and encouragement to me and it has helped me in ways I never expected as a player. Also, presently I should perceive when the time has come to end my serious profession."

However, it wasn't simply Wimbledon that Federer overwhelmed. He also won the US Open multiple times back to back from the year 2004 to 2008, six back-to-back Australian Opens, and as well as one French Open. That end, he said, will come at the impending Laver Cup on Sept. 23-25 in London. He referred to that as "my last ATP Visit occasion," and said, "I will play more tennis later on, obviously, however only not in Huge home runs or on the visit." He referred to it as "a mixed choice, since I will miss all that the visit has given me, and yet, there is such a huge amount to celebrate. I see myself as quite possibly one of the luckiest dividual on the planet today. I was born with a unique talent to play tennis, and I did it at a level that I never expected.

That doubtful span started at age 16 — very nearly 17 — in July 1998 in Gstaad, Switzerland, with a 6-4, 6-4 misfortune to Lucas Arnold Ker of Argentina, and finished at age 39 — very nearly 40 — in July 2021 at Wimbledon, with a 6-3, 7-6 (7-4), 6-0 misfortune to Hubert Hurkacz of Poland. In the middle between, misfortunes weren't a lot of the point as he won 103 competitions, second in male history just to Jimmy Connors (109). He turned into the main player with the entirety of the accompanying (and that's just the beginning): two back-to-back years coming out on top for three significant championships (2006-2007 and he additionally won three out of 2004), four successive years bringing home two significant championships, 10 straight significant finals, 23 straight significant elimination rounds (and 46 on the whole), 36 straight significant quarterfinals (and 58 everything considered).

He turned into the main male player with eight Wimbledon titles, with that Middle Court his haven even close to the Australian Open (six titles), the U.S. Open, and the French Open. He played a portion of the game's most worshipped matches, including his five-set exemplary bringing down of Pete Sampras in the 2001 Wimbledon fourth round at age 19, his five-set misfortune to Rafael Nadal in the 2008 Wimbledon last (broadly viewed as the best match at any point played), his five-set prevail upon Andy Roddick in the 2009 Wimbledon last that went 16-14 in the fifth (and pushed Federer past, Sampras, with a then-driving 15 significant titles), his five-set prevail upon Nadal in the 2017 Australian Open last that undeniable a renaissance for Federer and his five-set misfortune to Novak Djokovic in a 13-12 fifth-set sudden death round at the 2019 Wimbledon.

It was at Wimbledon, as Center Court gave him open cheers that had worked to blasting through such countless years, that he made his last uncommon air title bid. It included his two everlasting adversaries. He crushed Nadal in a highbrow four-set elimination round and lost that fifth-set sudden death round to Djokovic, who had battled off two match focuses nine games prior. Toward those opponents and others, he said in his declaration, "We pushed one another, and together we took tennis higher than ever." When they started, Sampras drove the way with 14 significant titles, and at this point, Nadal has 22, Djokovic 21, and Federer 20, with Djokovic's number restricted part of the way by his powerlessness to play a competition given his choice to swear off immunization for Covid.

"I wish this day couldn't ever have come," Nadal wrote in a message on Twitter. It's a horrible day for me and other sports all over the world. It's been a delight yet in addition an unbelievable honor to impart such an extremely long time to you, living such countless astounding minutes on and off the court." Following that horrifying misfortune to Djokovic, Federer showed up, faring significantly in three: the 2019 U.S. Open quarterfinals, the 2020 Australian Open elimination rounds, and the 2021 Wimbledon quarterfinals. He reported his most recent knee medical procedure in pre-fall 2021, pulling out from that U.S. Open all the while, then started a time of nonattendance which delivered his retirement declaration obvious.

That nonappearance followed a goliath abundance of presence. In the entirety of his standard bursts into the thin finishes of draws, he become a backbone before the world's eyes, which appeared to recognize in him something past the successes, past the ambassadorship that saw him calmly handle many years of information meetings in three-section portions highlighting three dialects, and past the sportsmanship that won him grants.

They talked frequently of a mathematical delight in his game until, after some time, it became conceivable to detect the "RF" covers of his image in metros from Seoul to Dubai to New York, among numerous different spots. Right off the bat, the tennis observer Mary Carillo alluded to Federer's style as "making soufflés out there." The famous French player Fabrice Santoro, near retirement at age 36 in 2009, thought back across a long vocation and said he'd never envisioned seeing anybody play tennis in the way Federer played it. The long-lasting French player Richard Gasquet, in a meeting with L'Equipe in 2021, fixed Federer as the highest level of player because, whatever the numbers, the style, and the beauty at which he played the game, made him essential.

The child of a South African mother and Swiss dad, Federer started at the Social Club Old Young men in his local Basel,

Switzerland, a simple club in tree-lined roads to which Federer's mom, a part, brought her child, then, at that point, matured 8 or 9, and shared with chief Madeleine Baerlocher, "I have Roger here. Might you at some point train him?" In his retirement declaration, Federer alluded to having been "a ball kid in my old neighborhood of Basel," yet one with now a universe of fans.

He discussed playing in "more than 40 distinct nations," referred to it as "so profound and mysterious that maybe I've previously carried on with a full lifetime," and expressed, "In particular, I have felt staggeringly invigorated."

Printed in Great Britain
by Amazon

86449747R00020